DISCARDED

W9-CJW-249

ST. PATRICK'S DAY

New and Updated

BY GAIL GIBBONS

HOLIDAY HOUSE
NEW YORK

To Barbara Walsh

**Special thanks to Dr. Sarah Waidler
(Lecturer, New York University)**

Text copyright © 1994, 2023 by Gail Gibbons
Illustrations copyright © 1994 by Gail Gibbons
All Rights Reserved
HOLIDAY HOUSE is registered in the
U.S. Patent and Trademark Office.
Printed and bound in September 2022
at Toppan Leefung, DongGuan, China.
www.holidayhouse.com
Second Edition
1 3 5 7 9 10 8 6 4 2

Library of Congress has cataloged the prior edition as follows:
Gibbons, Gail
St. Patrick's Day / written and
illustrated by Gail Gibbons. — 1st ed.
        p.   cm.
ISBN: 0-8234-1119-2
1. St. Patrick's Day—Juvenile Literature.
[1. St. Patrick's Day.] I. Title.
GT4995.P3G53 1994 93-29570 CIP AC
394.2'62—dc20

ISBN: 978-0-8234-5339-9 (second edition hardcover)
ISBN: 978-0-8234-1173-3 (second edition paperback)

St. Patrick's Day is celebrated each year on March 17th.

This holiday is celebrated by the Irish and other people in many parts of the world. They honor Saint Patrick, the patron saint of Ireland.

Saint Patrick lived many years ago. He was born in Britain hundreds of years ago and raised in a Christian family. His parents didn't name him Patrick. Some people believe his name was Maewyn.

When he was about sixteen, he was kidnapped and brought to Ireland where he was made a slave. His captors forced him to herd sheep. He prayed that God would help him. Six years later, he escaped.

After finally arriving back in Britain, he lived quietly, thought, and prayed. He realized what he wanted to do. He had dreams of returning to Ireland to teach the people about God.

People called scholars have been writing about Patrick throughout the years. They tell us that he may have studied religion in France, and we know that he became a priest, and then a bishop.

At last, Bishop Patrick's dreams came true. He sailed back to his country and began preaching. He built churches and schools all over the country. People noticed his kind ways and trusted him.

Bishop Patrick spent the rest of his life caring for the Irish
people. They loved this kind man.

People honor Patrick on March 17th because he died on that date. Years later, he was made a saint . . . Saint Patrick.

Today, many things are done to celebrate this holiday. People go to church to give thanks to Saint Patrick for his work in Ireland.

People have fun, too. They dress in green to honor an ancient Irish custom. Hundreds of years ago, the people of Ireland burned branches with green leaves and spread the ashes in fields to make them fertile and green. To wear green is to honor Ireland, the Emerald Isle.

Decorations are put on doors and windows. Shamrocks appear everywhere. The shamrock is a plant that has three leaves and looks like clover. It is the symbol of Saint Patrick as well as of Ireland.

Leprechauns are remembered on St. Patrick's Day. Long ago, some Irish folk believed in these little magic creatures. It was thought if you caught a leprechaun, you could make him lead you to a pot of gold. *Leprechaun* comes from the Old Irish word *Luchorpan*, meaning a magical little creature. People believed they were only as big as your thumb.

There is the shillelagh, too. In Ireland, many years ago, there was an old oak forest called Shillelagh. The Irish liked to own a "sprig of shillelagh," a short oak club from the forest. Often, people decorate shillelaghs with green ribbons.

The harp is one of the oldest musical instruments and has been popular with the Irish people since early times. It serves as another St. Patrick's Day decoration.

On St. Patrick's Day, people may give cards to their families
and friends.

People also make cakes, cookies, and goodies such as
Irish soda bread to share with others.

Some people wear green carnations or pin shamrocks to their clothes to celebrate the holiday. Others give flowers.

There may be St. Patrick's Day plays, too.

Some families and friends have quiet times together in remembrance of Saint Patrick. Often there are meals to share.

St. Patrick's Day parties are given, too. It is fun to sing
Irish songs and dance Irish jigs.

In many places, there are St. Patrick's Day parades. Flags
flutter in the wind. Pipers and fiddlers play Irish tunes.

There are green hats, people in costumes, green banners
. . . lots of green!

The first time St. Patrick's Day was celebrated in the United States was in 1737 in Boston. Each year, the Irish and many other people love to celebrate St. Patrick's Day.

For many people, it is a day for worship and for celebration,
and if you're not Irish, to feel a little bit Irish!

Saint Patrick and the Snakes

It is said that Saint Patrick got rid of all the snakes in Ireland. By beating his drum, he frightened them into the sea. Today there are no snakes in Ireland.

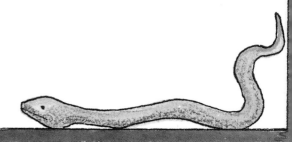

Saint Patrick and the Poison

Some people say that a wizard tried to kill Saint Patrick by putting poison in his drink. Saint Patrick quickly turned it into ice and tossed it from his cup.

Saint Patrick and His Cloak

It is said that Saint Patrick had a friend who borrowed his cloak. There was a big fire where the friend was staying, but he was not hurt because he was wearing Saint Patrick's cloak.

Saint Patrick and the Shamrock

Saint Patrick used the shamrock to explain to people about the Holy Trinity— one God in three divine beings: the Father, the Son, and the Holy Spirit. Growing at his feet was a shamrock. He used this plant to explain three in one— one stem with three leaves.

31333051274767

Saint Patrick and the Fish

Another legend is that each year on March 17th, fish rise from the sea. They pass before St. Patrick's altar in Ireland and then disappear back into the sea. This may be a reason people often eat fish and chips on St. Patrick's Day.

Saint Patrick and the Sunset

It is said that the sun didn't set when Saint Patrick died and that it shone in the sky for twelve days and nights.